A Compilation of
Higher Thoughts
II

Ascend

Bryan Thorne

A Hidden Script Production

A Bryan Thorne Creation

Part Of The Bryan Thorne Collection
Both are imprints of Lost Crown Republic L.L.C.

Cover Art & Illustrations by Bryan Thorne.

Copyright © 2013 Bryan Thorne

All rights reserved.

ISBN: 0615776078
ISBN-13: 978-0615776071

Higher thoughts ||... I found beauty the in illusion.
This is more than gibberish I'm introducing.
Came for the throne, I set a movement.
I believed it and did it.
Still remember they said I couldn't do it.
Let's travel to the land of Higher Thoughts.
Welcome to my galaxy.
You've just ascending to astounding heights.
—Enjoy the view, walk my path,
You just watch, you don't have to get trapped with me.
I'm chasing success and I have failure chasing after me.
—I have no time for procrastinating.
I've been mass creating. product fascinating.
Altitude past the stratus.—Sailing.
I'm half man, half my creator.—I woke up I'm in the matrix.
They didn't think I would make it.
They didn't think I would make it.

CONTENTS

1 Theta Lau Creta Airlines

2 Road to Success

3 The Black Tablet

4 The Documentary

5 Legendary

6

7

8 Afterlife

9

10 About The Author

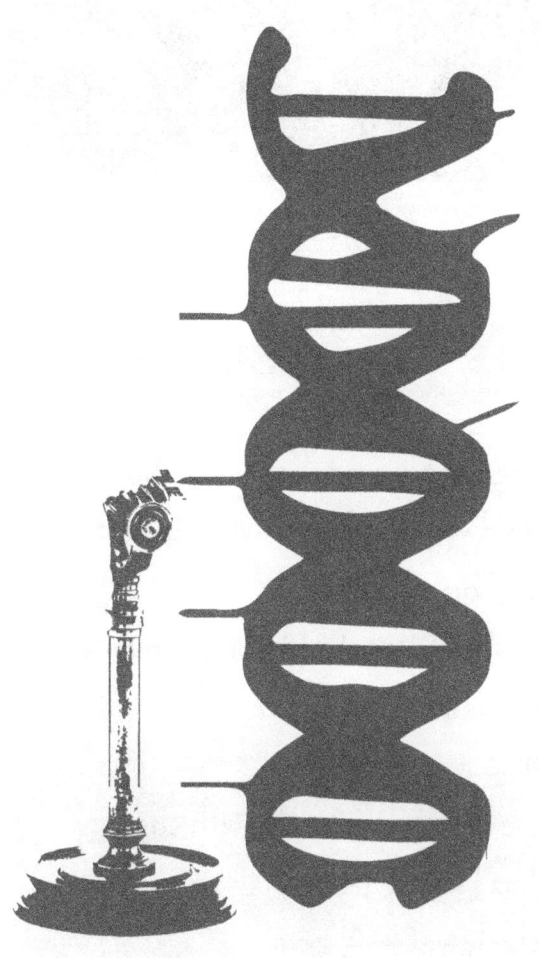

THE AIRPORT

Baggage

I. At my age, you'd probably think
II. that I'm new to this. But what your viewing is
III. Higher Thoughts.
IV. —They should probably come with a stewardess.
V. I take a qualitative approach to this.
VI. I make the rules with this.
VII. I can't be told what to do with this.
VIII. Founded Lost Crown,
IX. I found a jewel.—A gem.
X. Now I'm dripping and dropping them.—Offering.
XI. Only right I came right back after takeoff.
XII. —Before I landed I knew I'd be taking off again.

XIII. **Higher Thoughts.—**I been showing symptoms since
XIV. Kenan & Kel **after school and lemon heads.**
XV. Couple old friends think I changed up because
XVI. I came up with a dream that I didn't think
XVII. Need remain be made up.
    XVIII. **I know they mental enslave us.—King**
    XIX. **Free labor never repaid us.—King.**
XX. So I stayed up every night until they came true.
XXI. My apologies. but things like that can change you.
XXII. Have to get rid of the baggage its drains you.
XXIII. Change is good, but if you change improve.

Greetings treasured patron, and welcome back to Theta Lau Creta Airlines. It's been a while but I feel time has only made this voyage more memorable.

To My Opposition

I. "Oh, You write now?... Big deal.
II. I've been number one with **these words I jot**
III. Since I **swerved the block** in my big wheel.
IV. Running around in my diaper,
V. Momma yelling for me to sit still.
VI. Now when they poor they're pure

VII. —They've been remodeled, refined, and distilled.

VIII. Did you catch that?
IX. The ball has been thrown and I smacked that.
X. Your still running around in the in-field.
XI. You can keep running it's out of there.
XII. You'll never catch up I'm not from here.
XIII. You don't write enough,
XIV. you don't know how a pen feels.
XV. Along came Polly, It's time to meet the parents.
XVI. —Like Ben Still.
XVII. Running out of papers, need to re-up.
XVIII. I write faster than you read,
XIX. So there's no way you can keep up.
XX. I'm already in the fast lane, your just making it past
XXI. the speed bumps. Are you comparing us together?
XXII. How dare you take a spaceship
XXIII. And compare it to a feather?
XXIV. Your illegitimate I'm legitimately ill.
XXV. I son you authors, and in my death
XXVI. they'll present an empty will.
XXVII. You're afloat in troubled waters.
XXVIII. You're a fish with fifty eels.
XXIX. Before you begin, you should have seen what

XXX. You were in for.
XXXI. You just saw me kill like ten poets.
XXXII. You're about to witness ten more.
XXXIII. I don't have a weak spot, I'm sorry if I hit yours.
XXXIV. It's time for me to start my reign.
XXXV. I'm sorry if I end yours.
XXXVI. Now that I have your attention,
XXXVII. Tell me what are your intensions?
XXXVIII. You can either surrender yourself to
XXXIX. My service or I'll attend yours.

Quality

I. This here is poetry In a fine state.
II. I'm forever faded. I'm elevated.
III. I'm in a whole different mind state.
IV. But if I must say so myself
V. It was a fine race.
VI. You gave your all but I gave more.
VII. So if yours are sore...
VIII. You can rest assured that mine ache.

Wrath of a Forgotten King

I. I'm in first, I been first.
II. I'll never stop until my pen burst.
III. —Never stop writing. I'll be dead first.
IV. **No one writes as much as I.**
V. Don't compare me to the birds,
VI. They don't fly above sky.
VII. Life throws you ups & downs,
VIII. **I'm trying stay above tide.**
IX. If it's destined that we must collide.
X. I'll be right here yelling surfs up.
XI. **Sentence structure is unorthodox**
XII. But I'm doing it on purpose.
XIII. I'm the reigning king, I chased my dream.
XIV. In a land where there unheard of.

Ok, now that's enough of that... I was so caught up with that discussion I almost missed my own plane. I'll see you at the terminal.

Terminal 19

I. Welcome to Theta Lau Creta Airlines
II. Hop in the air's fine.
III. I live here, the air's mine.
IV. I write here. I like air.
V. I come here in my spare time.

Flight 93

I. Higher Thoughts. Might fall out orbit like comets.
II. No time for a troll in my comments.
III. I'm just being honest.
IV. Look as this script, it's gifted... it's polished.
V. I got in line with my consciousness.

VI. I've been climbing for a while now.
VII. Look around all I see is airplanes.
VIII. Attendant she asked if I'd like a drink,
IX. We're flying so close we could share planes.
X. Aviator Bryan's on his way to the cockpit.
XI. This is you pilot, your safe here I promise
XII. I could get you there in my sleep. I could pass
XIII. Through the clouds in 40 seconds right now

XIV. Even if I closed my eyelids.
XV. My friends are so close to the pilot,
XVI. That they feel like it's their plane.

The plane starts shaking. Lights start flashing overhead. Then an announcement begins: All passengers return to your seats, strap in, and remain calm. We seem to be experiencing a little turbulence.

After the release of my first book I felt as if no one gave it the credit that it deserved. I submitted for countless awards and a boundless number of contest and won absolutely nothing. From the pain and the anger of being disregarded a monster was created.

I. I know this might be your first look
II. I need for you to catch up.
III. My thoughts move way too fast to back up.
IV. This is my world.
V. There's work to be done.
VI. —Most people don't believe
VII. In what I work to become.

VIII. Nothing New

I. There's nothing new under the sun.
II. And all of the other number grew
III. from under the one. If you want beef,
IV. It's a half pound piece resting under my bun.
V. I'm feasting.—A beast that grew from nothing
VI. but a bundle of crumbs. I spit like I threw lemons
VII. On a bundle of tongues.
VIII. Write like I'm printing on treasury notes
IX. ISBN's.—I got the Treasury on hold.
X. Talk like I walked in the bank.
XI. —Told the cashier to bundle the funds.
XII. All I know is how to chase a goal,
XIII. Told myself I'm gone do what I love.
XIV. When I came for top I was broke.
XV. —Even back then I knew what it was.
XVI. Top 5 percent is a given.
XVII. Rise.—I ascend I get lifted.

XVIII. Chasing dreams, that ain't nothing new.
XIX. Dedication isn't comfortable.
XX. Bet on yourself. Invest in yourself.
XXI. I know it sound selfish, it is.
XXII. But if you want the truth...
XXIII. Ain't nobody else gone do it for you.
XXIV. You can ask them, that ain't nothing new.

I made it out of that stage and threw away my resentment. All holding on can do is prolong your moving forward. I realized there is a journey to greatness. A road that all hero's must travel. And that disappointment was just one of the many setbacks that were sure to come. But this is what I wanted. This is what I asked for. This is what I sing up for when I set out on a quest to become Legendary.

Legendary
Road to Success

I. Not sure why it surprised me,
II. The road to greatness never eases.
III. Fame at will may come and go,
IV. I pray my ambition never leaves me.
V. I hope wishes proceed me.
VI. **I know the human mind's limitless.**

VII. Built my own path, laid it brick by brick.
VIII. I had faith in my dream I insisted it.
IX. I clear my mind to think positive,
X. I know what my true potential is.
XI. I know that stat's on my industry.
XII. Can you define what ascension is?

King Bryan, your highness, your majesty. But if your dream comes true, then what becomes of your reality? I just hope I Don't become a causality... of the Momentum.

Momentum

I. I know I'm destined for greatness,
II. I just wonder if I'll make it there.
III. I know that heaven is real,
IV. I just wonder if I'll make it there.
V. I got product, I'm stocked up, I stay prepared.
VI. I been stuck to the page, like I'm stapled there.

VII. I've been building my momentum.
VIII. If you don't hustle you not living.
IX. If you're not selling than your buying.

X. No such thing as standing still...
XI. If you're not rising than your dipping.

XII. Hate it or love this, it's needed.

XIII. Our art's on the brink of extinction.
XIV. Creativity is at an all-time low.
XV. The artist an endangered species.

The Ills of the Life

I. Sand expanding in the bottom hourglass,
II. So before the rest spills.
III. I'll use every breath left I perfect my skills.
IV. I know my genius in past has been arrested,
V. I suspect the government has the rest killed.
VI. **I'm a Hustler.—African American Activist.**
VII. Those before me similar thoughts
VIII. Are associated with assassination.

Bryan Thorne

Nightmares

I. My dreams have turned to nightmares,
II. I've become content with them.
III. There not that bad,
IV. and by the time wake I won't remember them.
V. I'm more scare of killing a dream
VI. Than living a nightmare.
VII. Checking off goals like they're Nike Air's.

VIII. Don't worry, I don't sleep much anyway.
IX. **I put grinding over dreaming any day.**
X. Success is just a process.
XI. You don't have to do it all today,
XII. You're a success long as you're making progress.
XIII. Before I give up,
XIV. I rather be thrown in a lake with a loch Ness.
XV. The world is foul but so am I
XVI. —I just hope that the penalties offset.
XVII. My word flow is resembles a faucet.
XVIII. Until I'm dead I'm not missing a deadline.
XIX. I'm on the phone with success.
XX. When you called you got a dead line.
XXI. Ever since I was a kid I never did believe in bedtime.

XXII. Life is like walking a tight rope—it's a thin line.
XXIII. If being ill was illegal...
XXIV. I'd probably have about ten fines.

Ambition

I. I pray for opportunity... I would jump at the chance.
II. I can't go to games, I would jump out of the stands.
III. Jump on the court. I wanna raise a banner.
IV. You're a fan who just came to see the sport.
V. I play the game to ball.—I just came to see the court.
VI. I want to live my life on film,
VII. I should make a documentary.
VIII. Record all of the hurt, and tape all of the memories.
IX. I prey on the mentally tricked and feel awful.
X. The power circle is just me and my apostles.
XI. I'm dreaming of a distant world
XII. While sleeping upon the Apollo.

When your dreams come true... what do you dream about?

That's all I see when I sleep now—which I barely ever do. I haven't slept in about a week. My brain won't let me... it just won't shut off. I stay up all night thinking. But as rare as sleep is now, I'm just happy it still comes. But dreams don't... ever. I haven't dreamt in an amount of time that now exceeds that of my memory. This is the remnants of my last dreams. This is what it consisted of. I don't remember them now, but I wrote poems, I even drew. I'm not sure why, maybe subconsciously I knew it would be my last. Before that day it had been years since I drew. Previous to the dreams the last time I had drawn had been my freshman year at Ottawa Hills High School.

Maybe that's why I don't sleep. Maybe the lack of dreams make me not want to sleep. So while I'm awake I just work towards making the dreams I used to have come true. The poems I wrote I've realized told a story.
So what I give you, is the story of the last dream.

Higher Thoughts II

Complete Darkness.

I. How many nights must I dream the same dream?
II. How many night close my eyes, and see the same scene?
III. Ever since I was a kid when I went to bed
IV. My head keep repeating the same scene.
V. Different situations creating the same thing.
VI. Created it in real life ,the nest night I went to sleep
VII. And seen completed darkness.
VIII. Didn't remember a thing.
IX. —Living my dreams when I'm conscious
X. So when I sleep it complete darkness.
XI. Even at a young age trapped words and amazed.
XII. For the murder that he wrote and you all are now witnesses.
XIII. It's a closed case
XIV. They found the murder note to my competition.
XV. Couldn't keep it to myself I felt limited.
XVI. –Had to shared it with the world.
XVII. Even if it meant sentences.
XVIII. —Typed it up, printed it.
XIX. Couldn't enslave my creation...
XX. So I so I got it distributed.

The Last Dream

I. As I lay down and begin to slumber,
II. I lose all sound and begin to wonder.
III. The curtains open up, the beginning number.
IV. Its dark outside and it begins to thunder.

V. As I begin to drift off...
VI. **I feel so free to ascend and get lost.**
VII. When I sleep, it's like
VIII. I open up a chamber of secrets.
IX. A portal opens, exploding potions
X. Exploring emotions.—We all have angels & demons.
XI. I'm scared but won't wake up.
XII. —I'm amazed by the sequence.
XIII. Legendary.—Pool of immortality.
XIV. I ask you who better at craft than me?
XV. I throw these words paint so casually.
XVI. My ancestors accessed the galaxies.
XVII. Turn a blank page to a gallery.
XVIII. They fooled us all into thinking
XIX. That we didn't rule our own reality.
XX. Deceived our mental wealth

XXI. So we don't believe in self.

XXII. I captured a dream, had my last dream.
XXIII. I turn my last dream to a reality.
XXIV. I believed in me, increased my salary.
XXV. You could do the same if you attach belief.
XXVI. Put in time to achieve mastery.
XXVII. Don't mean to come off cocky but honestly
XXVIII. Those of my age are not in my lane.
XXIX. —Speaking modestly.
XXX. Ascension. Coming for all they predicted.
XXXI. Not fazed at all my resistance.
XXXII. On my wave I got momentum.
XXXIII. Third eye View high as birds eye's.
XXXIV. Ascended to absurd heights.
XXXV. Mentioned that I went to Alger Heights.
XXXVI. Thanks for purchase.—Come observe my rise.
XXXVII. Promise in turn a thousand gems,
XXXVIII. If you pay attention I'm dropping them.
XXXIX. I hope the right quote could spark a change.
XL. And inspire you to embark on reign.

Quest for the Lost Crown

I. What would you fight for...
II. What you love? Or who you love?
III. Looking back the series deeper than I knew it was.
IV. I had the idea for Higher Thoughts
V. Before I knew what the movement was.
VI. **They'd asked me why I write**
VII. **I told them "Do what you love.".**
VIII. Flow sick.—Make you lose your appetite.
IX. Tired of dealing with baggage,
X. Luggage won't fit if you don't pack it right.

XI. I live in a league of free thinkers.
XII. I put on a show with ease,
XIII. Only thing I need's the bleachers.

XIV. I'm my only challenge, I continuously beat myself.
XV. So many bruises & scars it hurts just to see myself.
XVI. Food for thought, read it aloud I could feed myself.
XVII. Rich in the mind.—Know it'll manifest
XVIII. & I'll receive my wealth.

XIX. I'm so cryptic. to read it is to visit
XX. A wall of pyramids and hieroglyphics.
XXI. I think I owe myself, to decode myself.
XXII. Because no one knows me like I know myself.

Master Craftsman

I. I used to speak a lot… now my pen speaks for me.
II. Back then I wanted to rap, now my pen records me.

III. Time is money, creating dreams can is expensive.
IV. When you find what you love,
V. In chasing it be relentless.

Gaze at stanza and all you see is crooked lines and spaces. And you might find it basic, but my words rhyme in places that in due time you'll find amazing. Now rewind my statement and read again and see what you see within.

Buried Treasure

I. If I told you the truth you would reject it.
II. You been mentally conditioned to reflect it.
III. Low self-esteem has my community infected.
IV. Every form of media's a different method.

V. I close my eyes to think open.
VI. I breathe notes, and see notions.
VII. My mind is a deep ocean
VIII. Where you'd find you could sink floating
IX. Thoughts will never be decoded.

I write down all the laws and recite them.
Memorize them.
You have to know them to defy them.

I moved away because they got nosey.
No one knows me on my island.

The Island

The island is my retreat. My escape from the rest of the world. The place I go to think. To everybody 61 that's feeling 16. To the very small child with the really big dream. To those who don't fit in and to any in-between. To the young at heart & the old at soul.
To those trapped in the dark that don't know their glow. This is hope.

Treasures from the Island

I. I learned a promise is only as good as it's kept.
II. The longest journey still begins with a step.
III. Take the "T" from won't & can't
IV. And you'll only see achievement.
V. Because anything is possible
VI. To someone who believes it.

VII. What is stress to one who knows how to relieve it?
VIII. What's an offense to a defense?
IX. An ambush to one who sees it?

Touch The Sky

I. Momma said "One day son, you'll touch the sky"
II. But all my cousins said I wouldn't
III. "cuz it's much too high."
IV. I said "I know what imam do today!"
V. —Phinneas & Ferb.
VI. Rode 6 escalators, grabbed plenty of the herb,
VII. Grabbed 18 pigeons, and twenty other birds.
VIII. Stood on top of ten giraffes and a couple hundred

Higher Thoughts II

    elephants.
IX. They said "You buffoon!"
X. I grabbed a balloon... **filled it up with helium**
XI. Hopped in my hot air balloon:
XII. Light it up, then sail.
XIII. Grabbed the herb out my pocket.
XIV. Spark it up... inhale.
XV. Then the people got smaller & the air got thinner.
XVI. I was next to a plane.—I hopped in and got dinner.
XVII. Then I touched a cloud...
XVIII. My finger almost poked through.
XIX. Laughed at all my cousins...
XX. Said "Momma you were sooo true!"
XXI. I made my momma proud
XXII. Looked down saw a crowd
XXIII. So I Jumped on a cloud, rode it around like Goku.
XXIV. ...Then the cloud broke and I started to fall.
XXV. Threw my hands toward the ground,
XXVI. yelled "Khama Hama HAAA!"
XXVII. Man 1: Look up in the sky!
XXVIII. It's a bird! It's a plane!
XXIX. Man 2: Wait... I think it's a Boy!
XXX. How absurd!
XXXI. How insane!

That's what they murmured on the day I touched the sky.

Dream Big

I. If you want something worth getting,
II. You should go and get it.
III. You're on your own nothing is owed.
IV. You don't go for your goals you're sure to regret it.
V. No matter what happens don't happen to forget it.

VI. They deserve it... if they made it, you encourage.
VII. Even if they had to make a song and couldn't sing...
VIII. Give them credit.
IX. They could be the worst player on the team...
X. Give them credit.
XI. Because they started with nothing but a dream...
XII. They believed in when they dreamt it.
XIII. When you find your purposes
XIV. No purpose to over think it.
XV. Try your hardest even if you get an "F" for it.
XVI. When your children have dreams
XVII. Please don't egg nor it.

XVIII. For a dream to hatch you have to build a nest for it.
XIX. If they makeup superhero's,
XX. Make up capes for them.
XXI. Invest in your children they are the way forward.

XXII. One day he could get a check for it.
XXIII. Don't take your kids life
XXIV. Thinking you know what's best for it.
XXV. If you see your kids dream in a vending machine
XXVI. If you see it's in the row left of "C3"
XXVII. Press "B4" for it.
XXVIII. You better press before it.
XXIX. Because you're in a press for time
XXX. It's running out, and you have to press before it.
XXXI. And if you can't afford it,
XXXII. Stick your hands in the bottom
XXXIII. Reach, and screech forward until
XXXIV. Your stretched before it.
XXXV. Fight as long as you live,
XXXVI. Let your dying breath be for it.
XXXVII. Get it or die trying let your death be for it.

And as long as I don't give up... I know what's waiting for me. On my island.

Island Girl

I. I'll have to learn how to use a ukulele.
II. My girl is always dressed in pieces of two
III. That are usually used for bathing.
IV. I have no plans on getting married...
    I see no point in waiting.
V. —Plus her body's so engaging.
VI. Her names engraved on my heart.
VII. —Which by the way is pacing.

The Island

I. It's a whole new world.
II. It's like a scene form a dream...
III. You must distance yourself from hate.
IV. I put a sea in-between.

V. Jealousy, greed, and envy...
VI. People whose minds were empty
VII. Their soul purpose was to end me.

VIII. Stagnant.—Mind state of statues
IX. Eyes green as goblins.
X. Their positioning brings problems.
XI. Have you noticed all the green of the sea
XII. Is at the bottom?

XIII. In the end, the inconvenient truth is:
XIV. If you don't pull a weed by the root
XV. Then it's useless...

XVI. If you cut back, the addiction still lingers.
XVII. When life pulls at you, you pull back...
XVIII. Strapped boots, aggressive stance,
XIX. And still fingers.

XX. Good vs. Evil is a battle of tug a war.
XXI. Who do you tug for?
XXII. When the bad pulls at you,
XXIII. you don't just tug back... you tug more.
XXIV. They don't agree, pull them to your side.
XXV. If their feet are planted and your slide...
XXVI. **Then sometimes... it's just best to let go.**

BLACK TABLET
The Forgotten City

Dedicated to a lost generation.

The Young Black Girl

I. Momma's been tripping lately, it's getting sickening.
II. She told me I can't date
III. Because she got pregnant at sixteen.

IV. You have to understand "Momma I'm not you!"
V. You didn't have your parents... Momma I got you!

VI. ...And you taught me right?.
VII. Every time I ever fell you caught me right?
VIII.

IX. Now I'm sixteen and I can walk on my own.
X. But even when I walk, I'm not walking alone.
XI. Your always right there with me...
XII. So it doesn't feel right yet.
XIII. I thought I was riding on my own...
XIV. You didn't let go of my bike yet.

XV. I love being under your guidance
XVI. But I'm breaking off.
XVII. I appreciate the training wheels
XVIII. But think it's time I take them off.

The Young Black Male

I. I still remember the stories you read me at night.
II. Can't lie, I cried when he read me my rights.

III. I used to get mad when you put me on punishment.
IV. —Now I'll be inside for the rest of my life.
V. Dad wasn't there, but I thank God
VI. For blessing me with you.
VII. But when nothing goes right,
VIII. what is there left for you to do?

IX. I accept the fact I did wrong.

X. 9-5 wasn't enough for us to live on.

XI. I know the town is full of gossip,

XII. I know what happens publicly.

XIII. When you walk outside

XIV. all you hear is people judging you and judging me.

XV. But I'm not here because of you

XVI. I'm stuck in here because of me...

XVII. I know your scared for me.

XVIII. And know you care for me.

XIX. But don't fear for me

XX. No tears should leak.

XXI. And don't you ever second guess

XXII. The job you did preparing me.

XXIII. Just remember that I love you

XXIV. Until next time that you hear from me.

The Misfit

I. These days everybody the shit...
II. I guess I'm just too fresh.
III. And everybody moving bricks...
IV. I guess I'm just too blessed.

V. But if I tell you that I did,
VI. Would you feel a little better?
VII. And does it lower my appearance
VIII. If my parents still together?

The Dime

I. Beautiful smile, make you wish
II. you could make her smile forever.
III. Make her say cheese might to take a little cheddar.
IV. Weather cash, credit, or debit.
V. She buy it, swipe it, and shred it..
VI. She's a spender.
VII. Watched basketball wives
VIII. & fell in love with the splendor.
IX. As long as you keep tender
X. you can be a lead contender.

XI. Be aware you need to keep her content.

XII. We want to attain her, she wants not to attain us.
XIII. We want to give her love,
        XIV. She just wants to be famous.

The Environment

I. The streets will swallow you whole.
II. Money is power, unconquered can devour souls.
III. The unsuccessful hold anger
IV. Towards those who succeed.
V. Doubters tend to send shade
VI. Towards those who believe.
VII. To bring others down makes them awful happy.
VIII. They see your close to the top,
IX. That's when their claws get snappy.
X. You're ok when you're at the bottom,
XI. Try to move up and they snatch you down.
XII. This what surrounds me. Vultures circling their prey.
XIII. When hate is all around you it gets hard to escape.

XIV. Handcuff the establishment.
XV. —And everyone staffed in it.

Legendary

XVI. So tired of being harassed against.
XVII. —All this hate got me feeling like the protagonist.
XVIII. Stashing these white faces,
XIX. You know they don't wanna see no one black with it.
XX. You know they hate a young black entrepreneur,
XXI. You know they hate to see a black activist.

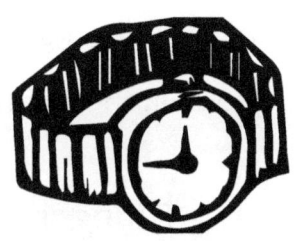

Timepiece

I. As I look at my watch that says "Made by hand."
II. I realize time doesn't exist... it was made by man.
III. Jay-z & Dame gave us a blueprint, I made my plan.
IV. I wasn't dealt the best cards.
V. —I dealt with it and played my hand.
VI. As I look at my watch that's says "Made by Hand".
VII. I brought it around the corner...it was made in Japan.
VIII. I can buy up the street what's not made in my land.
IX. But if I sell lemonade without a permit...

X. They could take my stand?

In the Undeveloped Rose Garden

I. I just made a garden.
II. You have no clue how much dirt it took.
III. I walk outside neighborhood get dirty looks.
IV. Grabbed a flower pot and I made my plant.
V. Yea, I clean up nice... but it's unappreciated.
VI. Now that's a line only the maid understands.

Hunger

XXII. Hunger comes from desperation.
XXIII. Sleeping dragon that you've let awaken.
XXIV. I wouldn't say I'm eating yet...
XXV. But I'm on my way I made reservations.
XXVI. The first rule of war is self-preservation.
XXVII. Know they self.—Self-education.
XXVIII. I own it all... independent like the declaration.

Trapped

XXIX. All I want is to be free.—I woke up I was back in.
XXX. I should have known, you can't walk out the matrix
XXXI. Once your jacked in.
XXXII. Being born black in America were trapped in.
XXXIII. —I'm just trying to prevail.
XXXIV. When bored I hop aboard my train of thoughts...
XXXV. They tell you that it's something in our DNA,
XXXVI. —Something in our cells.
XXXVII. We buy it when we can't afford it.
XXXVIII. See prices, but were so ignorant we ignore it.
XXXIX. For years we've been extorted.
XL. I'm tryna put the black dollar back in orbit.
XLI. Black Gold.—They don't know what IV is.
XLII. Black Gold.—They don't know what IV is.

Black Roses

XLIII. From the ghetto's rose meadows of rose pedals.
XLIV. Where waistlines expose metals which often explode.
XLV. Leaving cold statues of souls who's flow
XLVI. got lost in the mold. madness disguised as magic
XLVII. Turn clay into caskets.—What Harry Pottery.

XLVIII. How can a child grow on top of
XLIX. foundation that's tottering?
L. The corner has us cornered in.
LI. I don't want to be the coroner's friend.
LII. We walk a tight line never knowing the corners bend.
LIII. Handshakes exchange bagged death.
LIV. Strange men with battered clothes and bad breath
LV. Hairlines receded.
LVI. Hand outstretched as he approached.
LVII. Quick as he came he retreated.
LVIII. You know the procedure.
LIX. Every couple minutes repeat it.
LX. Sometimes want to turn off your phone.
LXI. —It keep ringing. I got to get it, I need it.
LXII. Black Widow's & black roses.
LXIII. Black windows, black Rolls-Royce
LXIV. Black employees, working sweating.
LXV. —Like black pastors. Preach.
LXVI. Welcome to the kingdom.
LXVII. I got to get it, I need it.
LXVIII. I been collecting my dues.
LXIX. I might pass collections before proceeding.
LXX. Thank you for coming this evening.
LXXI. "Get some money chase some dreams!"

LXXII. "Every day you'll see improvement,
LXXIII. Use it it'll keep you moving!"
LXXIV. "Action turn illusion turn to movement!"

LXXV. "We're all in constant vibration!"
LXXVI. "Come catch a vibe I've been waving!"
LXXVII. "We're all in constant vibration!"
LXXVIII. "Come catch a vibe I've been waving!"

Broken Society II

I. Women try to impress these men.
II. Men try to impress these women.
III. They buy outfits, they go out to fit in in.
IV. Long as it's new they don't even care if it fits them.
V. To them a helping hand is a hand out.
VI. They stand in line waiting for their chance
VII. To stand out.
VIII. In this broken society...

IX. I have keys to unlock and open society.
X. I don't have to chase.
XI. My vernacular already captured her.
XII. Till I run out of space, I'm not coming back to earth.

XIII. I've been chasing my dreams.
XIV. Met the girl of my dreams,
XV. And told her I'd have to get back to her.
XVI. Captured my dreams, now it's back to her.
XVII. If you ask me she is love.
XVIII. —None before her and none after her.
XIX. I set out to write a good book and I did it.
XX. She said it's good that it's good;
XXI. But she'd buy it either way
XXII. So she wouldn't care if it isn't.
XXIII. By the look of it I've been wining.
XXIV. The young boy from the mitten.—Fresh as a mint is.
XXV. In this...

B
R
O
K
E
N

S
O
  C
I
E
  T
Y

Word From The Wise

I. This is a word from the wise.
II. Word from the vine.
III. Words to the suppress, we gone rise.
IV. Only time.—It was written, must I remind.
V. Don't want to work to provide.
VI. Or wok to survive. I'll work to devise
VII. These words to remember. These words to revise.
VIII. These words to see stars,
IX. These words to see skies.
X. Words to evaluate the culture,
XI. Mediate, and ease minds.—Words could freeze time.
XII. Me and the crew breaking news.
XIII. —Ron Burgundy time.
XIV. I do this so quick it gets boring sometimes.
XV. I don't sleep much,
I. Even if I do I get up early most times.

King B

II. Flow so cold.—In degrees it would snow.
III. Higher III.—Indeed this is growth.
IV. Placing dreams in quotes, achieved the unachievable.

V. First taste of bread, knew I needed loaf.
VI. First seen bookshelves, knew I need a row.
VII. Script presidential.—No need to poll.
VIII. Ill so cold, don't need no post.
IX. So much show don't need no host.
X. Geese I'm cold. I'm knee deep in the sea.
XI. She just leaked, I mean she's soaked.
XII. —I might need a boat.
XIII. Young Harry Potter.—I might need a cloak.
XIV. Catch me ink to sheet making magic happen.
XV. I been at sea since three years old.

Young Woman

I. "Young woman, come here and here
II. These stories of old. Said the older woman.
III. This is what the young woman told.
IV. "Old lady patient and weak,
V. But the young woman bold.
VI. I'm tired of old woman and old woman scold."
VII. Old Woman responded: "Patience is strength,
VIII. Have you ever see this old woman fold?
IX. Old woman young woman once,
X. A young woman cold."

Stories of Old

I. In the black of night... I've seen visions decay.
II. A sea of dreams dried up and withered away.
III. Watched as souls flickered away like bad lights.
IV. As the moon shines, through the black of the night.
V. Fumes in rotation like satellites.
VI. —In the black of night.
VII. Now picture this in the back of your mind.
VIII. Odysseus. With emphasis
IX. On the different pigment.
X. Our people have a story too. We had a journey too.
XI. And this is how it went.
XII. Just trying make it home,
XIII. No justice in the system we're in.
XIV. We're caged in, we've been fenced.
XV. Life's been no gentlemen's Inn.
XVI. They rule with low self-esteem.—It's a prisoners den.
XVII. Low living conditions. Low mental conditions.
XVIII. The majority become the conditions their given.
XIX. The heart of the city was barley an inch.
XX. No heart in the city.—The city is tin.
XXI. The mayor's Darth Vader. –Committee is Grinch.

XXII. I've seen judges throw books at illiterate children.
XXIII. Hatred is starting, and pity is benched.
XXIV. And love and compassion are sitting with him.
XXV. Surviving is tough.—A diamond in rough.

XXVI. One day, in the dark of the night…
XXVII. At the park by the slide
XXVIII. Young boy asked to take a loan.
XXIX. He was told this was no place for kids
XXX. In the dark of the night.
XXXI. So listen here young woman.
XXXII. There are things you must know to become woman.
XXXIII. Until a young man has ring on her finger,
XXXIV. young man shouldn't touch young woman.
XXXV. He should protect her, he should love young woman.
XXXVI. He should love himself as should woman.
XXXVII. Good man deserves good woman.
XXXVIII. Woman defines herself.
XXXIX. Woman should not let others make her.
XL. Woman make world go round.
XLI. Don't believe me ask mother nature.
XLII. Find a young man who makes his father proud.
XLIII. A young man who does his mother favors.

XLIV. Young girl, quit wasting your time.
XLV. He don't love you now, he won't love you later.
XLVI. Cut from the cloth my Grandmother tailored.
XLVII. I won't buy a house unless it trumps the neighbors.
XLVIII. It should come with waiters, and a couple acres.

Fourth and Inches

I. This is a glimpse from a blimp.
II. My flows over heads, Coach putting me in.
III. —I don't sit on the bench.
IV. Sipping my sip with a fist full of Grinch.
V. Dividing attention.—I'm highly addictive.
VI. They noted how polished the scripture is.
VII. I'm mining my gold, and minding my business.
VIII. They pick me to win, I'm in line with predictions.
IX. Chasing my dreams.—I'm right within inches.
X. All these books, might supply an exhibit.
XI. I did it.—I needed it, I get it.
XII. When you vacation know somewhere
XIII. Your competitions in the gym.
XIV. Seasoned indeed, look how genius his script is.
XV. If he didn't do it, he's obscenely descriptive.

XVI. Dreams seemed impossible,
XVII. So let's redefine possible limits.
XVIII. I thought it, I dreamt it.
XIX. I woke up, I plotted and did it.
XX. Hope they don't stop me, don't got no prescription.
XXI. I'm practiced, I'm faithful.
XXII. —At birth was attached to an angel.
XXIII. Thoughts so high I went from
XXIV. Bumping birds to ducking mars.
XXV. When crossing planets your path
XXVI. Can get tangled amongst the stars.
XXVII. Making money with the team,
XXVIII. We get it all and we keep it all.
XXIX. —We don't need to see how much is ours.
XXX. Speak so deep it touches hearts.
XXXI. If it's fourth and inches, I'm taking chances.
XXXII. —If it's fourth and inches, get 4 yards.
XXXIII. MC Hammer.—They not touch ours.
XXXIV. James Brown.—With his cape down.
XXXV. Ball like Jordan.—I'm space bound.
XXXVI. I dismantled the Analyst.
XXXVII. Catalytic way I'm breaking down.
XXXVIII. I've chased dreams. That's in the latter since.
XXXIX. —Can't run after something you've chased down.

XL. If it's fourth & inches then I'm going for it.
XLI. —I don't waste downs.
XLII. The no contesting me.
XLIII. I'm at the top and no one's next to me.
XLIV. If you're doing that for me, you can stop.
XLV. —It's not impressing me. I have a few options.
XLVI. Fixing different dishes.—That's the chef in me.
XLVII. They tried to make the same meal,
XLVIII. But they're disrespecting my recipe.
XLIX. They attempted to whip up the signature dish
L. Got in over their heads.—Couldn't finish the mix.
LI. Words hit so hard, you'd turned over the ball.
LII. —There's no fifth and an inch.
LIII. I like options and presented a few.
LIV. She looked bubbled in like a test to me.
LV. Yes it's he. Yes it's king
LVI. Flow colder than the depths of the sea.

The Diamond Theory

I. Our movement is a crew ship in lucid water.
II. Watch it wave up.
III. The hate causes us to be cautious.

IV. So into my dreams, I get nauseous when I wake up.
V. Momentum building income,
VI. Offers come but we resent them.
VII. A million couldn't sway us.
VIII. Knock it off.
IX. You won't even get across the moat to knock.
X. I have my castle gate up.
XI. Why do they hate us?
XII. Because the women that they're laid up
XIII. With blow stray kisses and lick lips like they ate us
XIV. And we tasted good. Pretend they don't care,
XV. But when they find out they won't take it good.
XVI. Comparing us to them,
XVII. is like comparing oak to basic wood.
XVIII. We're pennies thrown over the well.
XIX. Every time I'm in a store, I want to pull over the selves
XX. And put my own up.
XXI. I'm going up to put where I roam up.
XXII. —Like the coliseum in Rome does.
XXIII. Get my money up I'm traveling.
XXIV. —I'll be in Rome more than the Pope does.
XXV. Blood on the leaves got me feeling like Yeezus.
XXVI. **—We came a long way from when they owned us.**
XXVII. Chained up physically & mentally.—They broke us.

XXVIII. In the end this is what it comes to.
XXIX. Those who break the chains are runaways.
XXX. Will you want to stay, or will you run too?
XXXI. Hut one, Hut two.
XXXII. What do you do when they ball is snapped
XXXIII. And you have nowhere to run to?
XXXIV. With a defense so aggressive
XXXV. That they're on the fence of trying to hurt you.
XXXVI. When it's too late turn back,
XXXVII. Even though you know you want to.
XXXVIII. Blood in the breeze got me feeling like Jesus.
XXXIX. –I say they hung him like a slave,
XL. They save they hung him like a thief.
XLI.
XLII. What do you do when it's forth and inches?
XLIII. Do you bring out specials teams?
XLIV. Or lay it all on the line, and force it inches?

The Documentary

I. Hurry up and grab a night light.
II. Paul Revere.—We're about to take a night ride.
III. To city's way more beautiful at night time.
IV. Grab your kids, tuck them in,
V. and tell them *Night Night*
VI. Here's an introduction to my life.
VII. If your life was a song how would the lyrics go?
VIII. Something sweet, something deep,
IX. or something spiritual?
X. Someone asked me what that meant to me.
XI. And my life was never the same mentally.
XII. So while I have you here with me
XIII. I share with you my life.

XIV. All my thoughts and all my memories.
XV. Higher Thoughts.—The Documentary.

The Profession

I. I hop out with my suit on. I move so professional.
II. You blow on soup... Well I just blew a bowl of vegetables.
III. I'm living on the moon... You only see the bright side.
IV. With these words I'm an artist infusing colors like I tie-dye.
V. Hi Bye. Hello and Good Morning.
VI. Days come & go. Some days come with mourning.
VII. I get blazed, grab some ink, and start recording me.
VIII. This is my lane... so when you drive here drive accordingly.
IX. Come to Lost Crown we professionals.
X. We're on our run it's exceptional.

Lessons & Levels

I. To you it probably feels like I made it in no time...
II. No watch. I should of made it years ago.
III. Wasn't the right time.—Broke watch.

IV. Money is how you spend it, time is how you use it.
V. Success is never ending.—It's a lifestyle.

VI. This is how you do it, the first step is a vision.
VII. —Turn your dreams into a movement.
VIII. Fear is just an obstacle.—An optical allusion.
IX. Give the your people something they can use,
X. Give them something that can improve them.
XI. Don't be confused...
XII. If you're not winning then your loosing.
XIII. Lessons & Levels.—I bring my art to confessional
XIV. My campaign making a motion.
XV. —It's still progressing now.
XVI. Lost Crown run getting excessive now.
XVII. We demand our own section.
XVIII. I'll only sign authors
XIX. that bring their own separate crowds.
XX. Lessons & Levels
XXI. Lessons and levels.
XXII. What else can I tell you? How else can I put it?
XXIII. Name a game without levels to it.
XXIV. Elevator way I level through it.
XXV. Everything you go through it's a lesson to it.
XXVI. Lessons & Levels.

Never give it anything less than your all.
You're going to make mistakes, just make sure there's a lesson involved.

The only way people won't Forget me is if I do something worth remembering. When I'm gone, you will remember me. Don't forget I said that.

The Evolution of Bryan Thorne:
Legendary

I. This was written in light of what's to come...
II. In light of what I've done.
III. In light of the things you haven't seen.
IV. I might release a book every month all 2017. King
V. Reign in the end will be legendary.
VI. I could to this till foreverary.
VII. Novels something to be marveled at.
VIII. I got a comic book series that marvel status.
IX. Come work with me, join the team.
X. I know Lost Crown will change the world.

XI. I have a book case on my wall in my room.
XII. Filled with original volumes.

XIII. Dress up these words they in costumes.
XIV. Jotted mounted on Mount Olympus,
XV. I need the gold, king he has goals.

XVI. Dreams came to life like Lightyear on Toy Story.
XVII. If I'm not flying I'm falling with style.
XVIII. And from these type of heights,
XIX. That might be a while.
XX. I'll be a legend by the time I touch the ground.

The Love

I. This is what I love. It's hard for me **not** to do this.
II. Do it for money but the truth is I would chose this.
III. I'll continue to do this until my pen is in my hand,
IV. And my mind is where the moon is.
V. Nine time out of ten...the bride is where the groom is.
VI. The body's in the coffin.
VII. —The coffin is where the tomb is.

Hansel & Gretel

I. My life fell victim of a vision.
II. I couldn't live if I didn't do it.
III. So I did it and I left a trail on the road.—it was breaded.
IV. There's a gap between you and your goals.
V. If you take action you can bridge it.
VI. It's a long fall and the water below is frigid.
VII. But I had to get it.

VIII. I leave a piece of me in each piece I write.
IX. And if you piece them all together

X. you would see my life.
XI. Each a part of a voyage to greatness.
XII. Higher Thoughts.
XIII. —Wavelengths displayed on pages.
XIV. I'm a genius, me and Einstein were like minded.
XV. I take my lifetime and write lines.—Lifelines.

XVI. They say life's about the Journey.
XVII. This is a memoir for when I get there.
XVIII. I figure I'll be thankful that I laid tracks.
XIX. So that one day you may find me...
XX. Or that I may find my way back.

King B The Original

I. Sometimes I don't like to write,
II. But this is what I was made for.
III. He only made one me,
IV. I know he could have made more.
V. Most people have one heart,
VI. But to me he gave four.
VII. Poetry, music, and art.—One rests inside my pen.
VIII. Rest assured this craft is destined to ascend.
IX. My chest is left with none.

X. That's why my pen feels, while my chest is numb.
XI. I'll breathe through my words.
XII. When there's no air left in my lungs.

Two Of A Kind

I. We speak in harmony, we don't rehearse it though.
II. We often fight on how a verse should go.
III. I love my thoughts, sometimes I feel
IV. As if were not the same person though.
V. So the product that you see
VI. is a product of two me's.
VII. In the same way that six is a product of two threes.
VIII. Wrote my life for you to read it.
IX. I infuse blue & black ink.
X. My mind starts racing like an athlete—Track Meet.
I. All alone. Just one me,
II. But I write like it's a lot of us.
III. I pull strings, and knot them up.
IV. I'm here to take the game and lock it up.

A Tale of Two

V. I show you both the good and the faults in me.
VI. I wouldn't be anywhere if
VII. I still cared what people thought of me.
VIII. Still climbing.—At the top, I have a spot to keep.
IX. Toss and turn hard I'm too awake to sleep.
X. Pursuing my dreams.—Have a pace to keep.
XI. I didn't lose my mind, it was stolen from me.
XII. Just like my freedom.—No doors opened for me.
XIII. They treat the black man in America like terrorist.
XIV. Distribution of Wealth.—Look at the disparity.

XV. They say they hold the throne, it looks vacant to me.
XVI. What you call hard work is a vacation to me.
XVII. This is me in my prime I'm optimal.—Optimus.
XVIII. Two-legged race I have eight.—Octopus.

Work Your Craft

I. I glide alongside my pen and I don't plan on landing.
II. I jumped into the sky, my feet don't plan on planting.
III. These books were my Plan A.
IV. I Never made a Plan B.
V. Ying & Yang
VI. If I was going to succeed at anything, surely this would have been it.
VII. My mind shifts as every sentence gets indented.
VIII. I haven't seen anyone write like me
IX. Since the pen has been invented.

Insomnia

I. My brain is too far gone to be repaired.
II. If I don't have the lead, then I don't think it's fair.
III. Why don't I sleep?
IV. Go ask the tortoise why he beat the hare.
V. I know my day is coming,
VI. I just need to keep prepared.
VII. I cause panic like the Winslow family

VIII. Whenever Steve prepared.
IX. I been the best since the years
X. When leave it to beaver aired.
XI. I want to watch a movie, but that won't get me paid.
XII. —So I slave on.
XIII. I'm building my momentum on this jungle gym I play on.
XIV. I could build my own world with some Lego's
XV. & some Cary-On's.

XVI. You can't make coffee unless you grind it up.
XVII. Even a jewelry box won't play unless you wind it up.
XVIII. I rocked and rolled with the punches.
XIX. —Like a beetle. I'm addicted.
XX. But don't confuse with the slave of a needle.
XXI. This is the carcass...
XXII. Of an artist who's been enslaved by his easel.
XXIII. I'm sitting at my drafting table
XXIV. I'm crafting a masterpiece,
XXV. I'm stirring my tea with an ladle.
XXVI. I know my path is rocky, still I'm rocking like a cradle.
XXVII. I'm growing up fast, like the stalk from the fable.

I. As of late I don't sleep much.
II. Every day you lose 8 hours,
III. How do you expect to keep up?
IV. I have a dream, it's reason why I'm awake now.
V. —Space bound. My dreams move at light speed,
VI. I'm in high pursuit as I chase down.
VII. Take a blank page and create places all my own.
VIII. Previously only known to imagination.
IX. My tomorrow is no mystery.
X. I'll be chasing Dr. E.am,
XI. We have such an extensive history.
XII. Everyone else is sleep.
XIII. And honestly I should be sleeping too.
XIV. But you can't build a castle with a leaking roof.
XV. The rain will just keep seeping through.

The Attainment of Greatness

I. Don't tell me that I'm too young.
II. You can either let me in or I'll break in...
III. Choose one. Take a chance, you might fail...
IV. Hey, you win some and you lose some.

V. You can try to slow me down, either way I'll get there.

VI. Won't give up crown? Either way we'll switch chairs.
VII. Before I run out of ideas, I'll probably tire of writing.
VIII. Before Floyd loses a fight
IX. He'll probably tire of fighting.
X. Well these lines are my ring,
XI. and these margins have me boxed in.
XII. The odds were I'd be locked up.
XIII. —Until I took my skills and locked in.
XIV. If I didn't sell my art, I'd probably be in a coffin.
XV. I don't know where life will take me.
XVI. I know it's a chance worth taking.
XVII. In the past it would stress me out,
XVIII. Now I've become accustomed to greatness.
XIX. I've been chasing dreams for so long
XX. I've become accustomed to track shoes.
XXI. I'd say this is great, if not then what would you call it?
XXII. I ask, though I don't care what your response is.
XXIII. "A rose by any other name…"
XXIV. By now that's common knowledge.
XXV. If my brain is just a sponge,
XXVI. Then I won't stop until I clog it.
XXVII. Decided to do what I love,
XXVIII. I've decided no way you could stop me.
XXIX. I dry lake's with my metaphors and lectures.

XXX. Words form my page turn a cane into a scepter.
XXXI. I drop jewels, put a quarter in the game
XXXII. Pulled the lever, whenever I play games I play to win.

Power

I. I grab my pen and I'm the creator.
II. I got the game sewed up.—I'm a tailor.
III. I'll never be a slave to another man's dream.
IV. I'm a owner, I'll never play for another man's team.
V. I have my own, why lust for another man's things?
VI. How many ways must I say no days off?
VII. I'm working from the a.m.
VIII. Until the sun takes its rays off.
IX. You're worried about employment,
X. Bosses don't get laid off.
XI. Your starring inside the mind of an alligator.
XII. My back is scaled like the spine of an alligator.
XIII. I just ordered a couple bricks
XIV. Think it's time to get the castle layered.

XV. When it comes to competition... I have none.
XVI. I wrote a book so fast that I forgot I had one.
XVII. My friends tell me I should stop writing and have fun.

XVIII. I've been up since 3 a.m. and haven't had lunch.
XIX. When I get it I'm going to splurge,
XX. Growing up I didn't have much.
XXI. I want my parents to live out the dreams
      XXII. That they had before they had us.

Unmoved

I. Before you judge know only fan has right to critique.
II. Only those who paid for ticket have right to a seat.
III. I used to want advance from a publisher,
IV. I didn't know I would have been a slave then.
V. Came on my own. You wouldn't know
VI. Way I rose to every occasion.
VII. I road though I was caged in.
VIII. I roam from days start to days end.—Restless.
IX. I'm a stray star that stayed when the rest left.
X. The most important view is your view of you yourself.
XI. When you don't care how you are viewed
XII. Is when your truest to yourself.
XIII. Get it right.
XIV. I'm the best line for line.
XV. I'm not really the gimmick type.
XVI. They can't come up with a plan of their own,

XVII. Sure they'll mimic mine's.
XVIII. I came and murdered the game,
XIX. I should be facing prison time.
XX. —Or at least given fines.
XXI. The way I speak is an amazing feat.
XXII. I run until my shoes deplete.
XXIII. Incomplete, I need to finish lines.
XXIV. I run until I've won, and proceed to visit finish line.
XXV. "If you're the best... why no awards?"
XXVI. I tell them give it time.
XXVII. Unbothered by unvalued opinions.

The Robins Cage

I. Too young to be Bruce Wayne,
II. I'm to closer to Robin's age.
III. So forget about the Bat Cave,
IV. Your all welcome to come over to Robin's Cage.
V. They say I'm too young to be the greatest.
VI. But when Batman was hanging from the ledge
VII. Was I too young for me to save him?
VIII. I didn't want to have to go there.
IX. Didn't want to have my own lair.

X. These next lines you might find a bit shallow...
XI. The bat signal shines pretty bright,
XII. But it's only the half the size of its shadow.
XIII. I play my role.
XIV. I play the back, but I'm next up.
XV. The day that Gotham needs me, I'll step up.

The Champion

I. Darth Vader, mind is on imperial.
II. Wake up every morning
III. Turning thoughts into material.
IV. Excuse the behavior, winners don't make excuses.
V. Never said he was better, just the aura he exuded.

I. Ascended Aspirations

II. My mind is completely insane, this is just a sampling.
III. This is not a full course meal, rather it's just a canapé.

IV. This book is nothing more than my attempt to capture my sanity.
V. Broken loose, it ran from me. So when the picture clicked...
VI. Instead it captured my vanity.

VII. Being broke is worse than breaking a bone
VIII. —No gristle, it fractures Family.

IX. Though I have a lot of fans,
X. As it stands I'm not a fan of me.

XI. I feel for victims of violence and pray for peace.
XII. That's just the man in me.

XIII. But I still roll with Malcolm X
XIV. —That's just the permanent tan in me.

XV. These words are the most addictive from of drugs.
XVI. And I'm cooking up a pan of me.

XVII. Authority problems, I kill captains.
XVIII. .... That's just the Peter Pan in me.

XIX. A disappointment I don't plan to be.
XX. The face of failure is a mirrored image I don't plan to see.

XXI. And that's no question...
XXII. N/A like a strand of D.

XXIII. command the easel easily.
XXIV. My bloodline rose from a land of G's.
XXV. I never follow the rest of the heard.
XXVI. (I abandon sheep)

XXVII. Haven't you heard I'm not from here?
XXVIII. I am an alien.... from planet me.

I.

The Definition of Bryan Thorne

II.

III. Don't read this too loosely, and don't take this too lightly.
IV. After this you won't forget me, I don't really care if you like me.
V. On a hot day I'm a High-C
VI. I stay icy as an ICEE or an iced tea
VII. H.N.I.C.
VIII.

IX.

X. And I stay H.I.
XI. And my mind stay H.I.G.–H.E.R.
XII. Coming live from the city of G.R.
XIII. With my pencil gripped my script so sick, you can visit it in the E.R.
XIV. Higher Thoughts on a Higher Regard.

XV. Compared to me, they're all small like 3 guards.
XVI. You run until you breathe hard.
XVII. I run until I fall. And then I run again,
XVIII. Even though my knee's scared.
XIX. I need an arm brace and a knee guard.
XX. My pen so slick I ski...
XXI. With the horsepower of three cars.
XXII. I shine as bright as 3 stars.
XXIII.
XXIV. Are you out your freaking mind?
XXV. How could him see me?
XXVI. My ice will take an eye out...
XXVII. Now him just CE.
XXVIII. Now him just CP...
XXIX. Add an R to that
XXX. That's elementary,
XXXI. But he just pre...
XXXII. Take the R back.
XXXIII. Because him just Jim, tryna bee like me.
XXXIV. But him gym, and me PE.
XXXV.
XXXVI. And Bee why?
XXXVII. Thee time
XXXVIII. They see "Y"
XXXIX. I did it.
XL. It'll be like I didn't.

THE END

A Note From The Author

If I am to be remembered, then I want the world to remember all of me. The good along with the bad. A lot of people don't understand that being talented is both a blessing and a curse. That being said, I don't want to lie about my life.

If you're going to tell a story, you have to tell the whole thing. Anything less than the truth is an insult to history. So if this book changes your perception of me... it was meant to.

Would you find it easier to kill a caterpillar or a butterfly?

What I give you is my life. Whether you like it or not this is the reality I live in. I'm not proud of my mistakes. This is not me glorifying drug abuse, addiction, violence, or anger.

This is just me telling the truth. Showing you the real me. This is me challenging you to find the beauty in the beast.

Before you judge me it's only fair you know all of me. Knowing all my faults... can you love me?

ABOUT MY BRUBBY

Bryan Thorne's **Higher Thoughts II: Ascend** is clearly a book best suited for Martians. His brilliant mind (yes brilliant, even though I hate to admit it) is in a different galaxy. He is beyond the Milky Way and all of us (not including myself) or most of you are still stuck there. At this particular point when Bryan was writing he had a breakthrough, more of an epiphany really. He realized he was untouchable, and self proclaimed he was the greatest. I personally think his already more than moderate sized ego grew bigger. Even if so, he may be on to something. What author, poet, artist, creative being do you know who finished 30 good books by 18. Yes thirty!

Bryan Thorne & _____ _____

(That was left blank intentionally.)

While you may still be digesting after reading food for thought...We must move on. Let me tell you more about the author. Bryan is like the great lakes that surrounds us here in Michigan. He is ever changing, and constantly moving to somewhere he wasn't before. His poems in **Higher Thoughts II:Ascend** are a natural evolution of his writings. If you read **Higher Thoughts I: Takeoff** then you can clearly see he packed more poems in fewer pages. And here and there you'll find his current personal thoughts/ back stories to his poems. Here you will find poems loved inspired, hate driven, mad, insightful, and outright genius. Who else can make all those different topics flow so effortlessly. The key for Bryan is just being himself. And if you're writing what's real and have the talent to write it in such a phenomenal way; how can whatever you write not work? One of my favorite lines from Higher Thought II Ascend is **"It takes a great man to look beyond the flaws, to see a beast and look beyond the claws."** That's truly who Bryan Thorne is, (not the beast) but he has the traits of what he is (a great, yes I said it) great man. He accepts everyone and gives everyone a fair chance, even if its underserved. Bryan is ascending as a poet, author, and person. If you ever meet him it will take you all of 2 minutes to realize he is on another level, really another planet. If you take Bryans Higher Thoughts I Takeoff and fuse it with more greatness the only outcome is Higher Thoughts II Ascend. I know what is coming next, and let me tell you, you cannot wait for it. And yes it does get better.(really you have no idea) So on your behalf I will urge him to release them sooner than later.

Until our next run in.
-Hattie Thorne

Bryan Thorne

Other Works By Bryan Thorne:

A Compilation Of Higher Thoughts
Vol. I: Takeoff

Bryan Thorne

Join Me…

Theta Lau Creta

Legendary

Bryan Thorne

www.ingramcontent.com/pod-product-compliance
Lightning Source LLC
Chambersburg PA
CBHW020016050426
42450CB00005B/498